Science That's Appropriate <u>and</u> Doable

This science resource book was written with two goals in mind:

- to provide "good" science for your students
- to make it easy for you

What makes this book "good" science?

When you follow the step-by-step lessons in this book, you'll be using an instructional model that makes science education relevant to real life.

- Your students will be drawn in by interesting activities that encourage them to express what they already know about a concept.

- Your students will participate in hands-on discovery experiences and be guided to describe the experiences in their own words. Together, you'll record the experiences in both class and individual logbooks.

- You'll provide explanations and vocabulary that will help your students accurately explain what they have experienced.

- Your students will have opportunities to apply their new understandings to new situations.

What makes this book easy for you?

- The step-by-step activities are easy to understand and have illustrations where it's important.

- The resources you need are at your fingertips — record sheets; logbook forms; and other reproducibles such as minibooks, task cards, picture cards, and pages to make into overhead transparencies.

- Each science concept is presented in a self-contained section. You can decide to do the entire book or pick only those sections that enhance your own curriculum.

For sites on the World Wide Web that supplement the material in this resource book, go to http://www.evan-moor.com and look for the <u>Product Updates</u> link on the main page.

Using Logbooks as Learning Tools

Logbooks are valuable learning tools for several reasons:
- Logbooks give students an opportunity to put what they are learning into their own words.
- Putting ideas into words is an important step in internalizing new information. Whether spoken or written, this experience allows students to synthesize their thinking.
- Explaining and describing experiences help students make connections between several concepts and ideas.
- Logbook entries allow the teacher to catch misunderstandings right away and then reteach.
- Logbooks are a useful reference for students and a record of what has been learned.

Two Types of Logbooks

The Class Logbook

A class logbook is completed by the teacher and the class together. The teacher records student experiences and helps students make sense of their observations. The class logbook is a working document. You will return to it often for a review of what has been learned. As new information is acquired, make additions and corrections to the logbook.

Individual Science Logbooks

Individual students process their own understanding of investigations by writing their own responses in their own logbooks. Two types of logbook pages are provided in this unit.

1. Open-ended logbook pages:
   Pages 4 and 5 provide two choices of pages that can be used to respond to activities in the unit. At times you may wish students to write in their own logbooks and then share their ideas as the class logbook entry is made. After the class logbook has been completed, allow students to revise and add information to their own logbooks. At other times you may wish students to copy the class logbook entry into their own logbooks.

2. Specific logbook pages:
   You will find record forms or activity sheets following many activities that can be added to each student's logbook.

At the conclusion of the unit, reproduce a copy of the logbook cover on page 3 for each student. Students can then organize both types of pages and staple them with the cover.

_____ 's Logbook

Animals without Backbones

Note: Reproduce this form for students to record knowledge learned during daily science lessons.

Name _____

This is what I learned about animals without backbones (invertebrates) today:

_____

_____

_____

_____

_____

_____

_____

_____

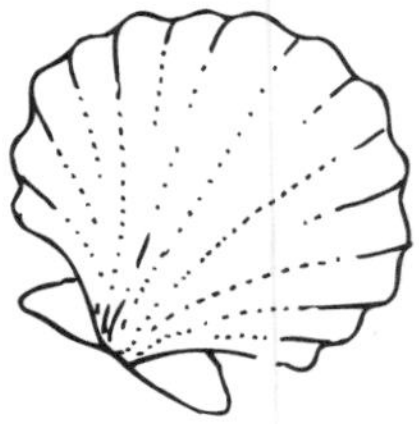

Note: Reproduce this form for students to record science investigations for their individual logbooks.

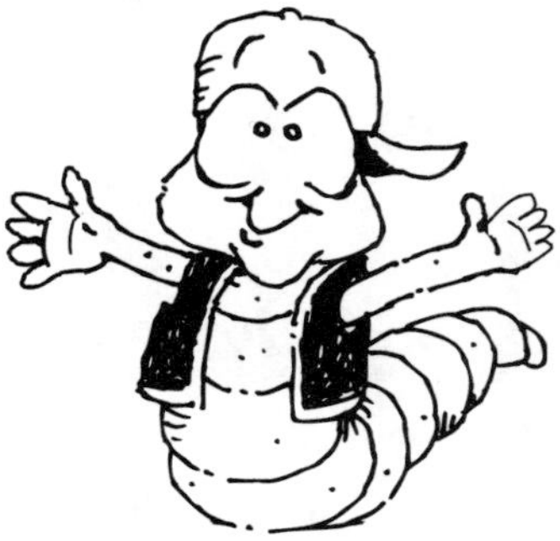

Name ______________________________

Investigation: ______________________________

What we did:

____

____

____

What we saw:

____

____

____

What we learned:

____

____

____

Animals without backbones are called invertebrates.

Backbone—No Backbone

- Make overhead transparencies of pages 8 and 9. Use these as you guide students through a discussion of animals with and without backbones.

  Begin by having students feel the bones down a partner's back. Ask, "What are you feeling? *(bones, skeleton)* What are those bones called?" If students don't know the answer, provide the term backbone. Explain that many animals have backbones, too. Ask students to name some of these animals. Show the overhead transparency of animals with backbones.

  Ask, "Do all animals have backbones? Can you think of animals that don't have backbones?" Show the transparency of animals without backbones. Point to each example and ask students to describe what they see. Explain that animals without backbones have a special name — invertebrates. (Not all students will remember this term immediately but will learn it through repeated use during the unit.)

- Begin a class logbook about invertebrates with a chart entitled "Backbone or No Backbone."

  Reproduce copies of the logbook form on page 4 for students to use when recording information for their individual logbooks.

Backbone or
No Backbone

Some animals have a backbone.

Cats, dogs, and horses have backbones.

Some animals don't have a backbone.

A worm doesn't have any bones.

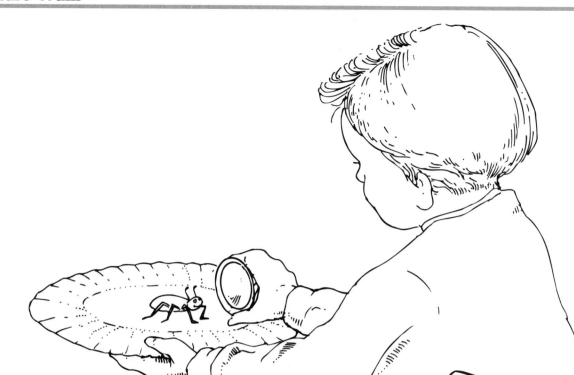

• Divide students into small groups — each with an adult helper. Provide each group with a plastic spoon (for picking up tiny animals), a paper plate (to hold the creatures while they are being examined), and a hand lens (for close looks). Each student will also need a record sheet (see page 10), a clipboard, and a pencil.

Have each group search for invertebrates in the school yard or a nearby vacant lot. (Emphasize that nothing is to be touched unless the group leader says it is okay.) Look under rocks, among plants, in cracks of tree bark and buildings, etc. (Remind students to be gentle as they handle these small creatures.) Pick up the invertebrate using the plastic spoon and place it gently on the paper plate. After examining the creature, replace it in the same area it was found. Students record each discovery on their record sheets.

Back in class, have students share the invertebrates they discovered. Make a master list of all the animals found for the class logbook.

• Reproduce page 11 for each student. They are to color animals without backbones and put an X on animals with backbones.

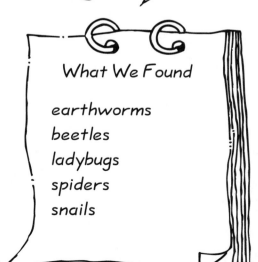

What We Found

earthworms
beetles
ladybugs
spiders
snails

Animals with a Backbone

Animals without a Backbone

Soft Invertebrates

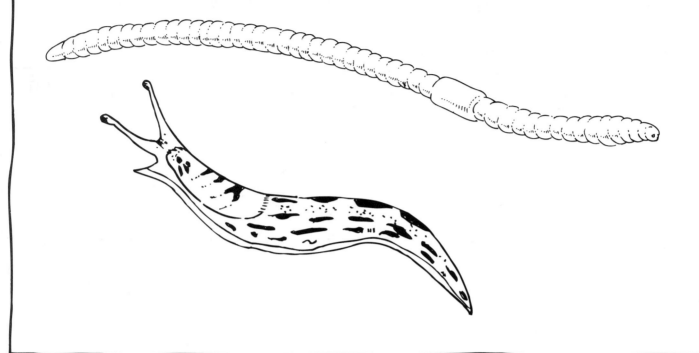

Invertebrates with an Outer Skeleton

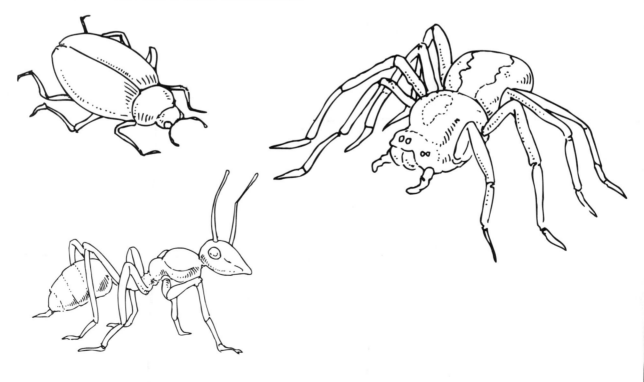

Animals without Backbones • EMC 855

Name _____

Nature Walk Record Sheet

Write and draw to tell about the animals you found.

draw and name the animal	where we found it	what it was doing

Name _____

Backbone or No Backbone

Color the animals that do not have backbones.
Put an **X** on the animals with a backbone.

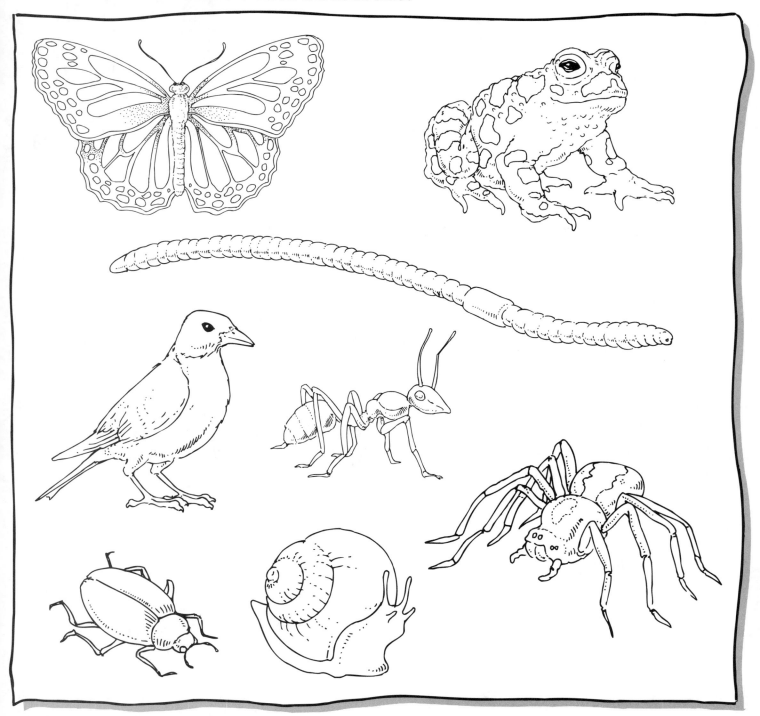

Invertebrates are classified by their body characteristics.

Teacher Preparation

Before beginning the rest of the unit on invertebrates, plan opportunities for students to observe animals.

- Plan field trips to places such as:
    a pet shop
    an aquarium
    tide pools

- Check your district audiovisual catalog for appropriate films and videos to share with the class as you study the various invertebrates.

- Set up containers of live invertebrates in the classroom. You will need at least two of the following:
    terrarium with land snails (see page 13)
    earthworm farm (see page 13)
    spider jar (see page 14)
    ant home (see page 15)

If possible set up a salt-water aquarium with small invertebrates, following directions from a pet shop.

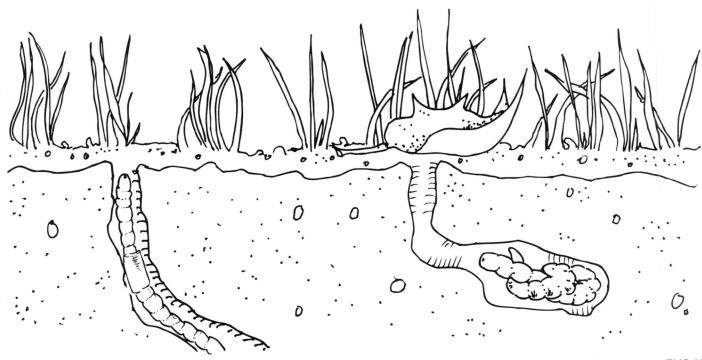

Snail Terrarium

Materials

- terrarium or gallon jar
- soil
- clumps of grass sod
- fine netting
- string
- snails

Steps to Follow

1. Place a layer of moist soil and small clumps of sod in a large terrarium.
2. Place half a dozen snails in the terrarium.
3. Cover the top with netting and tie it in place with string.
4. Keep the soil moist but not wet. Give the snails fresh food every day (flour paste, mashed potato, cabbage or lettuce leaves) and remove any old food. Clean the container every two weeks.

> If no land snails are available, set up a small aquarium or large jar with water snails purchased from a pet store.

Earthworm Farm

Materials

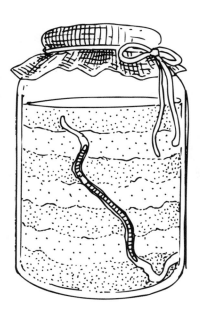

- large clear glass bowl or gallon jar
- soil
- sand
- decaying plant matter
  (collect from under a tree or bush)
- netting and string
- several earthworms
- black construction paper
  (large enough to go around the earthworm farm)

Steps to Follow

1. Fill the container almost to the top with alternating layers of damp sand and soil. Place decaying plant matter on top of the soil.
2. Place the earthworms in the container.
3. Cover the container with netting and tie it in place with string.
4. Keep the container wrapped in black paper when earthworms are not being observed. (Earthworms need a dark environment.)

Spider Jar

Prepare the jar and then collect a spider to keep in class temporarily. Look in dark corners, under rocks and logs, and in cracks in tree bark to find a nonpoisonous spider. Put only one spider in the container.

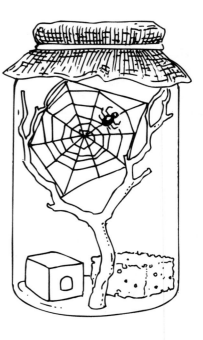

Materials

- clean, dry wide-mouth jar
- 6" (15 cm) square of nylon stocking
- stones, leaves, damp moss
- branching twig
- a rubber band
- a piece of sponge
- small box with opening cut in one side

Steps to Follow

1. Place the branching twig in the jar to support any webs. Place stones, leaves, and damp moss in the jar.
2. Put the small box in one corner to provide a dark hiding place for the spider.
3. Place a small piece of moistened sponge in the jar. This keeps the air in the jar humid and helps the spider survive its captivity.
4. Cover the mouth of the jar with a piece of nylon stocking. (This allows fresh air into the jar but prevents the insect's escape.) Wrap the stocking around the outside so that it covers the opening. Secure the stocking with the rubber band. Trim off the excess stocking.
5. If you plan to keep the spider more than a couple of days, you will need to provide live food for it. (Most spiders around our homes eat insects.)

> Although they may look fierce, most spiders are harmless to humans. However, the bites of the black widow or the brown recluse spider can cause illness and occasionally death. Before collecting spiders, familiarize yourself with the characteristics of these two spiders so they can be avoided.

An Ant Home

Collect ants by putting a moist sponge and some potato chip crumbs into a jar and placing the jar near an ant hill or across an ant trail. When the ants have entered the jar, cap it and take the ants to the ant home you have made by following the directions below.

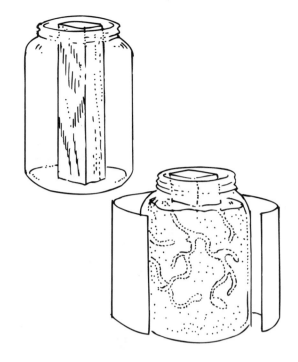

Materials

- a clean, dry wide-mouthed jar
- a block of wood almost as tall as the jar, narrow enough to fit through its neck
- a flat piece of wood small enough to fit in a baking pan
- rectangular baking pan
- a small piece of sponge
- sand
- water
- black construction paper
- potato chips
- ants

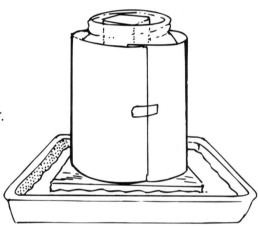

Steps to Follow

1. Stand the tall block of wood in the center of the unsealed jar.
2. Carefully pour sand all around the wood block until the jar is nearly full. Leave some room on top for the ants to pile up their tunneled sand. Dampen the sand with a little water and compress it.
3. Place a small piece of sponge on top of the sand and keep it moist with water.
4. Make a cylinder out of black construction paper to fit tightly around the jar. (The ants will tunnel quicker if they are in total darkness.) Remove the paper to observe the ants at work, but always replace it when you are done.
5. Place the jar on a block of wood in the center of the baking pan and put about 1/4 inch (.75 cm) of water in the pan. (The water in the pan will prevent the ants from escaping.)
6. Put a few crumbled potato chips on top of the sand in the jar and shake the ants you collected into their new home.
7. Keep the sponge in the ant home moist with water. Feed your ants a few crushed potato chips and a pinch of sugar once a week. Return the ants to the wild when you have completed your observations.

Observe Class Animals

- Ask riddles about the class invertebrates using their most obvious physical characteristics. Students are to identify which animal is being described.

    "This animal has six legs and antennae."
    "This animal has eight legs."
    "This animal doesn't have any legs."
    "This animal has one foot and feelers."

- Reproduce the observation record sheets for each student. (Use the generic form on page 18 for any animal, or the forms on pages 19–22 for specific invertebrates.) Divide students into small groups. Assign each group one invertebrate to observe. Provide hand lenses for each group. Explain that they are to record what they observe about the animal's appearance. Rotate groups through all of the class animals.

    Explain that students are to answer as many questions on the form as they can by observing the class animals. Any unanswered questions can be completed after students read the minibook on pages 25–27.

- Call students together and review what they observed. Record their discoveries on pages for the class logbook.

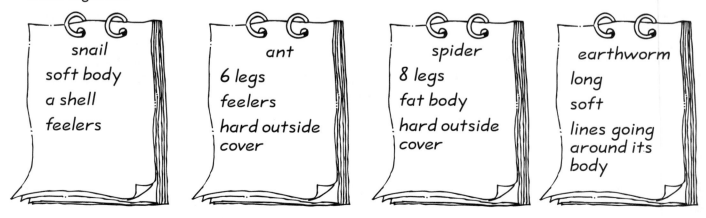

snail
soft body
a shell
feelers

ant
6 legs
feelers
hard outside cover

spider
8 legs
fat body
hard outside cover

earthworm
long
soft
lines going around its body

Compare and Contrast

- Reproduce the Venn diagram on page 23 for each student. (Or draw a large Venn diagram on butcher paper.) Select two of the class invertebrates to compare. Write one name in each circle. Work together to list characteristics that are unique to each animal and those that are common to both.

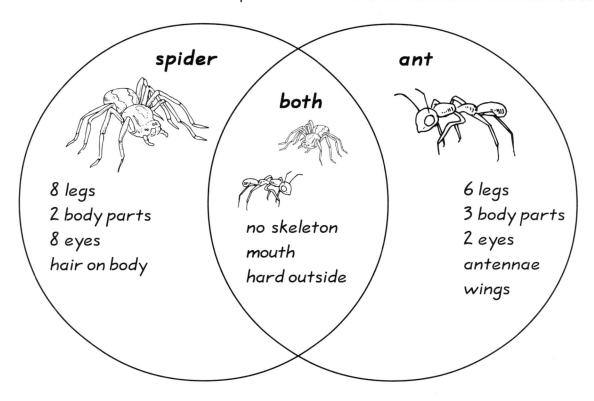

spider

both

ant

8 legs
2 body parts
8 eyes
hair on body

no skeleton
mouth
hard outside

6 legs
3 body parts
2 eyes
antennae
wings

- Reproduce the chart on page 24 for each student. They are to read each characteristic and then mark each animal it describes.

Animals without Backbones Minibook

- Reproduce the minibook on pages 25–27. Read together to review physical characteristics of land invertebrates. Make additions and changes to the class logbook pages written for each of the invertebrates (see page 16).

- Reproduce copies of the logbook form on page 4 for each student. Have them write what they have learned about each of the four types of invertebrates.

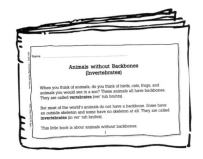

Note: Reproduce this form for each student to use as an observation record for any invertebrate.

Name _____

I Watched the _____
animal name

I saw these body parts:

_____

_____

_____

_____

Draw the animal.
Label its parts.

Name _____

Spider Record Sheet

1. How many legs do you see? _____

2. How many body parts do you see? _____

3. How many eyes do you see? _____

4. Does the spider have wings? _____

5. Does the spider have feelers on its head? _____

6. Does the spider have hair on its body? _____

7. Does the spider have a hard outside skeleton? _____

8. Label these parts:

    legs   abdomen   jaws
    feelers (palps)   spinnerets   eyes
    head and chest (cephalothorax)

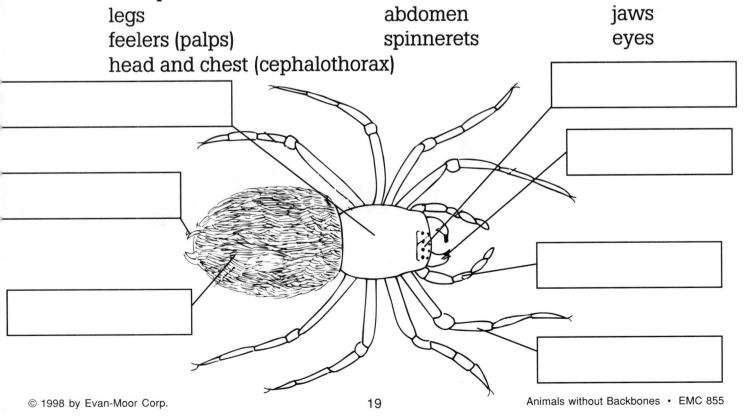

19
Animals without Backbones • EMC 855

Note: Reproduce this form for each student to use with page 16.

Name _____

Ant Record Sheet

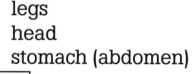

1. How many legs do you see? _____

2. How many eyes do you see? _____

3. How many body parts do you see? _____

4. Does the ant have wings? _____

5. Does the ant have feelers on its head? _____

6. Does the ant have a hard outside skeleton? _____

7. Label these parts:

        legs   eyes
        head   chest (thorax)
        stomach (abdomen)   feelers (antennae)

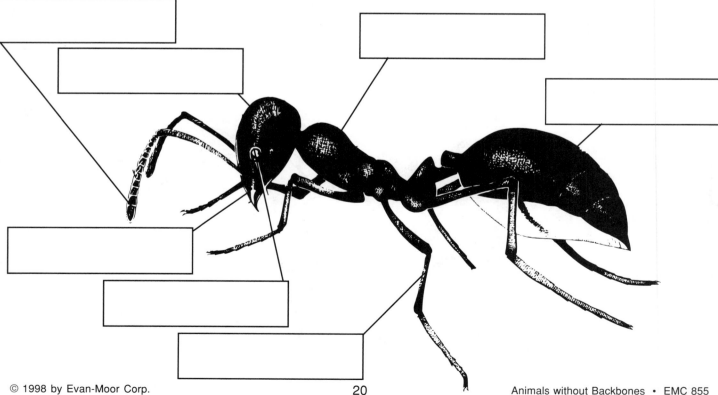

Note: Reproduce this form for each student to use with page 16.

Name _____

Snail Record Sheet

1. Does a snail have a head? _____

2. How many feelers do you see on the snail's head? _____

3. Where are the snail's eyes? _____

4. How many feet do you see? _____

5. What does a snail use to feel with? _____

6. How does a snail move? _____

7. Label these parts:

      foot   shell   feelers

      mouth   eyes   slimy trail

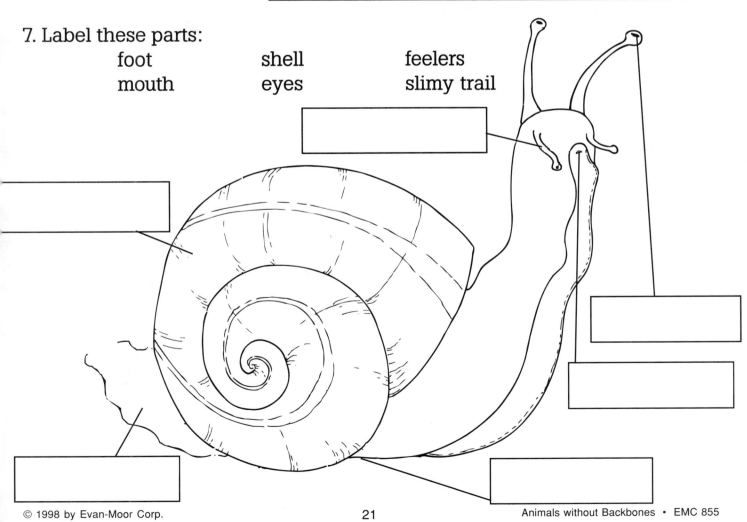

 Animals without Backbones • EMC 855

Name _____

Earthworm Record Sheet

1. How many legs do you see? _____

2. How many eyes do you see? _____

3. Does an earthworm have one body part or many body parts?_____

4. Does the earthworm have wings? _____

5. Does the earthworm have feelers on its head? _____

6. Does the earthworm have a skeleton? _____

7. Label these parts:

                mouth   head end

                tail end   a segment

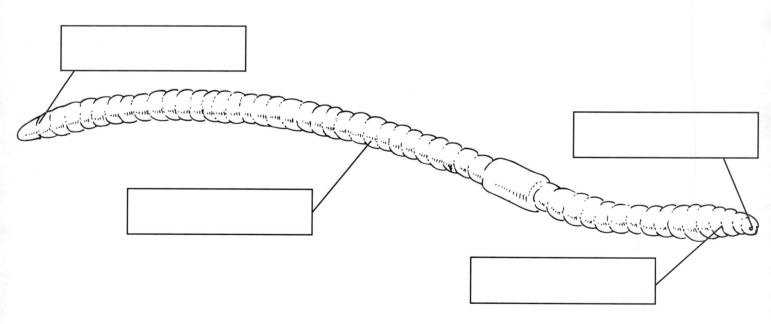

Note: Reproduce this form for each student to use with page 17.

Name _____

Alike and Different

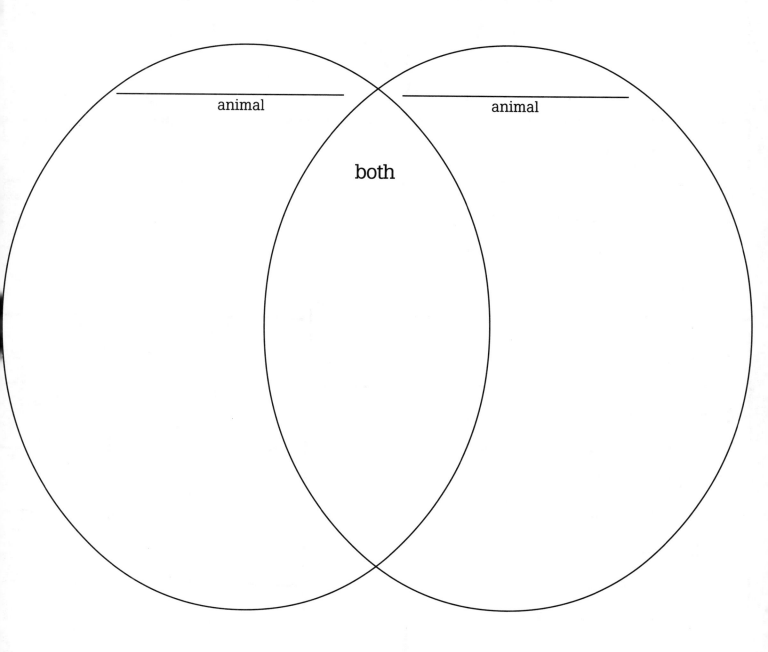

animal

animal

both

Name _____

Is It True?

Read each statement.
Put an **X** under each animal for which the statement is true.

	ant	spider	snail	earthworm
1. no backbone				
2. feelers or antennae				
3. eight legs				
4. body covered in a hard outside				
5. soft body				
6. hairy body				
7. six legs				
8. part of body in a shell				
9. wings				

Animals without Backbones • EMC 855

Name _____

Animals without Backbones
(Invertebrates)

When you think of animals, do you think of birds, cats, frogs, and animals you would see in a zoo? These animals all have backbones. They are called **vertebrates** (ver' tuh bruhts).

But most of the world's animals do not have a backbone. Some have an outside skeleton, and some have no skeleton at all. They are called **invertebrates** (in ver' tuh bruhts).

This little book is about animals without backbones.

1

Insects do not have backbones. They wear their skeletons on the outside. There are many different kinds of insects. They are different sizes, shapes, and colors. But they are all alike in certain ways.

Insects have six legs. They have two **antennae** on their heads. Most kinds of insects have two or four wings.

An insect's body is divided into three parts:
head
chest (**thorax**)
stomach (**abdomen**)

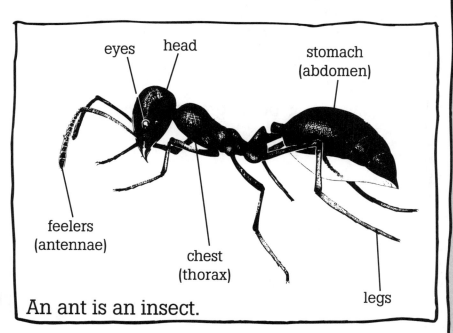

eyes   head   stomach (abdomen)

feelers (antennae)   chest (thorax)   legs

An ant is an insect.

2

Color the insects on this page.

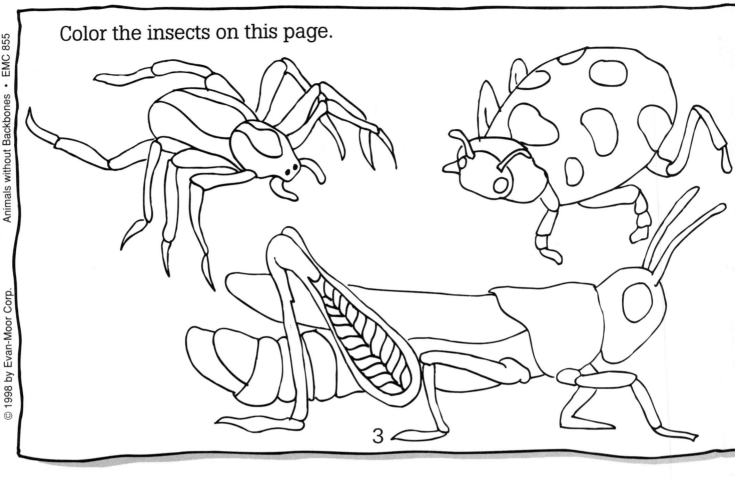

3

- -

Earthworms do not have backbones. They have long, soft bodies with no legs. Earthworm bodies have many parts (**segments**). Earthworms breathe through their skin. They don't have eyes, ears, or noses, but their skin can feel light. They feel movements of the ground.

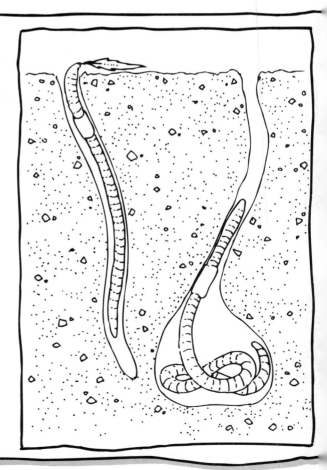

4

Spiders do not have backbones. Some are large and some are small, but they all are the same in these ways:

Spiders have 8 legs.
Most spiders have 8 eyes, too.
They have two main body parts.
They have hard skeletons on the outside.
They spin silk to make webs.
The silk comes out of tiny holes (**spinnerets**) in the spiders' abdomens.

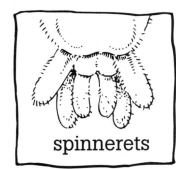

spinnerets

5

Snails do not have backbones. They have soft bodies with a head and one foot. There are two pairs of feelers on the head. One pair has eyes. The other pair is for smell.

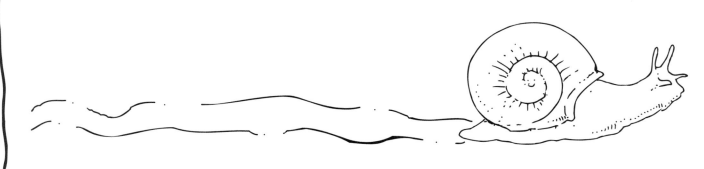

6

Most kinds of invertebrates live in the ocean.

Ocean Invertebrates

- Explain to students that all the animals without backbones they have studied so far live on land. Ask them to think about some animals that live in the ocean. List these on the chalkboard.

> fish   octopus
> crab   whale
> shark   starfish
> snails

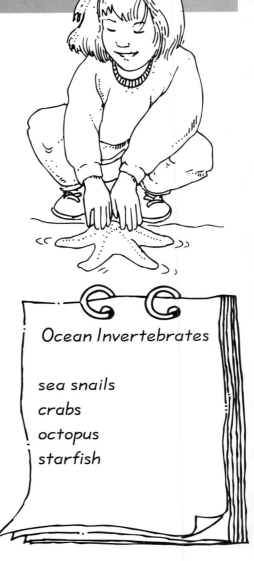

Ocean Invertebrates

sea snails
crabs
octopus
starfish

Have students decide which of the animals listed have backbones and which do not. (Encourage students to use the characteristics of the land invertebrates they know to help them decide — soft, squishy bodies; outside skeletons; bodies in a shell). Circle the invertebrates.

Explain that there are many more kinds of animals without backbones living in the ocean than living on land.

- If you did set up a salt-water aquarium, have students observe the invertebrates in the tank.

- Start a page entitled "Ocean Invertebrates" for the class logbook .

Take a Closer Look

- To prepare for this lesson, visit a fish market or supermarket to get samples of invertebrates for students to examine.

  small internal piece of cartilage — squid
  no bones — octopus
  external shells — oysters, clams
  external skeletons (exoskeletons) — shrimp, crabs

  Place each sample on a different tray. Cut open the squid and the octopus so students can see inside. Open the clam or oyster.

- Divide students into small groups. Allow each group several minutes to examine one sample to see if bones or a skeleton are present. Rotate groups until all groups have seen all the samples.

  Ask students to explain what is the same about all of these animals. *(None have backbones.)* Add these invertebrate names to the class logbook list.

Gather More Information

- Plan a field trip to an aquarium or to tidepools, if possible. If not, visit a pet shop that carries invertebrates for salt-water aquariums.

  Have students complete the "Field Trip Report" form on page 32 as they observe the animals.

  Back in the classroom, have students share what they learned about the different types of invertebrates. Add any new names to the "Ocean Invertebrates" logbook page.

- View videos about ocean invertebrates and read books such as *Life in a Tidepool* by Allan Fowler (Children's Press, 1996); *Mollusks* by Joy Richardson (Franklin Watts, 1993); *What Lives in a Shell?* by Kathleen Zoefield (HarperCollins Children's Books, 1994); and *Starfish, Seashells and Crabs* by George Fichter (Western Publications, 1993). Ask students to recall what they learned about the appearance of ocean invertebrates.

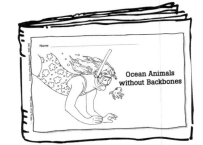

- Reproduce the "Ocean Animals without Backbones" minibook on pages 33–37 for each student. Read the pages together for review. Make additions and corrections to the "Ocean Invertebrates" class logbook page.

  Reproduce the logbook form on page 4 for students to write about ocean invertebrates for their individual logbooks.

Ocean Invertebrates Bulletin Board

Have students work in small groups to create a bulletin board showing some of the invertebrates they have learned about.

Background

Sketch a large tidepool background on a sheet of butcher paper. (The size will depend on how much display area you have.) Lay the sketch on the floor. Have small groups of students paint the rocks, sandy bottom, seaweed, and water. Let the background dry completely as students work on invertebrates to add to the bulletin board.

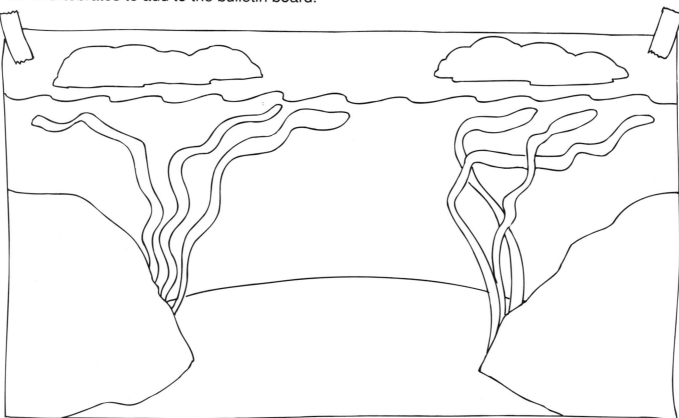

Divide the class into seven small groups. Assign one project to each group. Each member paints one or more of the assigned invertebrates (the number will depend on the size of the background). Provide trade books for students to use as sources for shape and color of the invertebrates. Allow the paintings to dry, cut them out, and glue them to the background.

Include the following;

- hermit crabs in different types of shells (glue to the sandy bottom)
- crabs (glue to cracks in rocks or sandy bottom)
- sea stars in bright colors (glue to rocks)
- sea urchins (make purple urchins; glue in clusters on rocks)
- anemones (some with tentacles out, some with tentacles in; glue in clusters on rocks)
- periwinkles, limpets, chitons (glue to rocks)

Note: Reproduce this form for each student to use with page 30.

Name ____________________

Field Trip Report

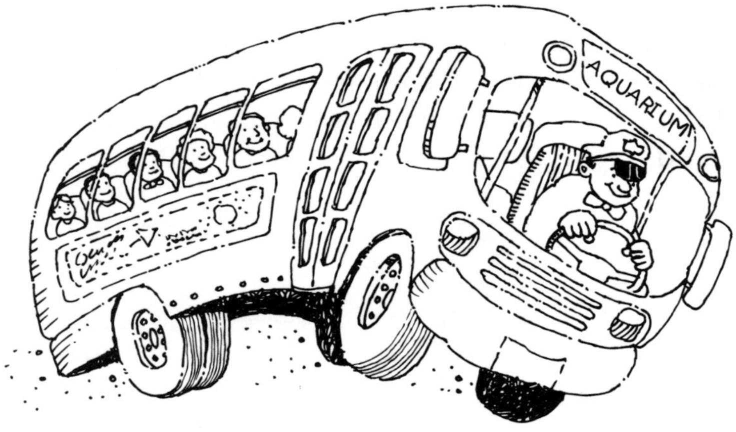

I saw:

____

____

____

____

____

I learned:

____

____

____

____

____

Name _____

Ocean Animals without Backbones

Most of the animals in the ocean are too small to see without a microscope. Some of them are made of only one cell. (Your body is made of millions of cells.)

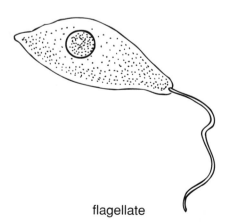

flagellate

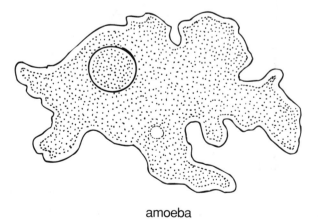

amoeba

These tiny animals plus tiny ocean plants are called **plankton**. Many other sea animals eat plankton for food.

1

Sponges don't have backbones. They look like "blobs" full of holes and tunnels. Some sponges grow like a crust on rocks. Some grow on animals' shells and get a free ride.

Sponges use little hairs to make water flow through their tunnels. The water brings in the plankton and oxygen they need.

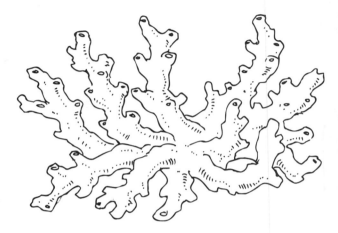

2

Anemones and **jellyfish** don't have backbones.

Jellyfish are not made of jelly, but they are soft and clear. A jellyfish has three main parts—an umbrella-shaped body (**bell**), a funnel-shaped tube hanging down (**mouth**), and long, stinging **tentacles** hanging down around the mouth.

Anemones (uh nem' uh neez) look more like flowers than animals. An anemone has tentacles around its mouth opening. The tentacles have stinging cells.

3

There are **snails** in the ocean, just like land. Sea snails have one shell. Some have a door at the opening of their shell.

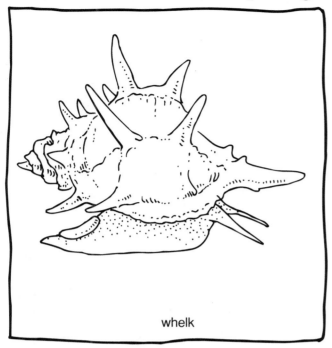

whelk

moon snail

Slugs look like snails, but they don't have shells.

Sea hares are giant slugs with feelers that look like rabbit (hare) ears sticking up.

Nudibranchs (nood' ih branks) are colorful slugs with gills sticking out of their backs.

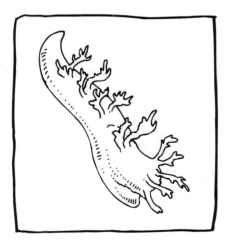

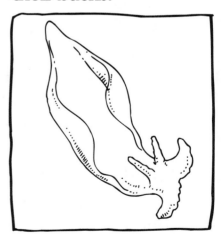

All three of these animals slide along on a "foot" that is like a snail's foot. Under a microscope, you can see that there are hundreds of tiny, hairlike parts called **cilia** (sil' ee uh) that move them along.

These ocean animals don't have backbones, but they do have outside shells.

limpet

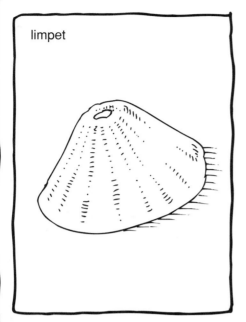

Some have one shell.

scallop

Some have a two-part shell.

6

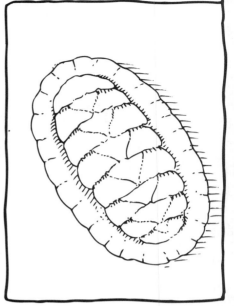

Chitons have a row of eight shells down their backs.

An **octopus** doesn't have a backbone. And neither does a **squid**.

Octopuses have eight arms, called tentacles, (ten' tuh kulz) with **suction cups** along them. Octopuses have round heads with two eyes. Their bodies are soft, with no bones at all.

Squid have eight long, pointed tentacles and two that are like long paddles. They have long, pointed heads with two eyes. Squid have a thin piece of cartilage, called a **pen** inside their heads.

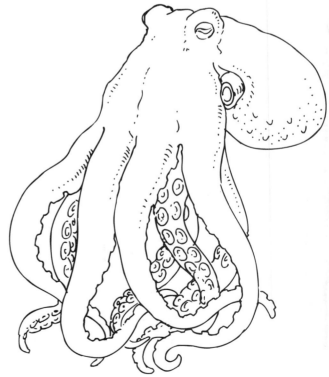

7

These ocean animals have hard body coverings and little tube feet.

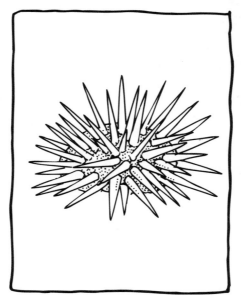

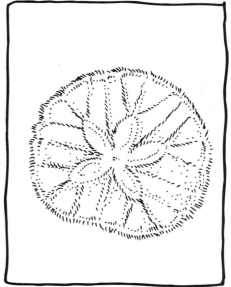

Sea stars all have five or more arms (**rays**).

Sea urchins are covered in spines. They look like little pin cushions.

Sand dollars are round and flat. They are covered in short, hairlike spines.

8

Like insects, these animals have their skeleton outside. They have **antennae**, or feelers. As they grow bigger, they crawl out of their old skeletons and grow new, bigger ones.

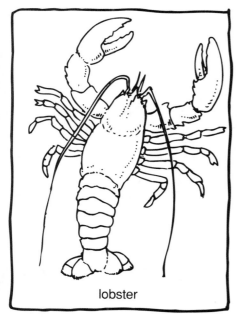

lobster

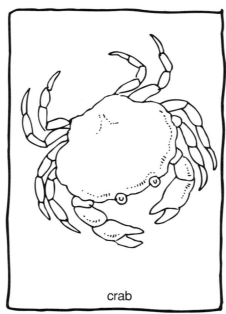

crab

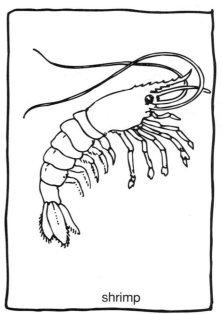

shrimp

9

There are several types of invertebrate life cycles.

Preparation

This section provides directions for following the life cycle of two invertebrates, a beetle and a butterfly, in your classroom.

Provide a selection of books showing life cycles for students to explore as they raise the invertebrates.

If possible, have students videotape each stage of the life cycle. Invite parents to see the video.

Egg to Beetle

• Introduce the concept of life cycles by having students share experiences with raising pets. Have them describe the physical changes they observed over time.

Explain to students that they will be learning more about the changes that happen as animals grow by raising some invertebrates in class.

• Purchase mealworm larvae at a pet store. Mealworm larvae form a pupae and then change into small, harmless beetles. The adults will lay eggs and then die. The eggs will hatch into new larvae. This process takes several weeks.

Materials

- mealworm larvae
- terrarium
- oatmeal, apple chunks
- paper towels
- observation logbook (see form on page 41)
- box lid, spoon, hand lens

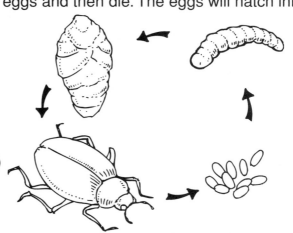

Steps to Follow

1. Put oatmeal, apple chunks, and damp paper towels in the terrarium. (Add additional oatmeal and fresh apple as needed.)
2. Add the mealworm larvae. They will eat the oatmeal and apple.
3. Watch the changes that occur as the mealworms grow and pupate. Feed the adult beetles dry dog food and vegetable bits. Each day, have a student observer remove a mealworm, place it on the box lid, and examine it closely. The student then completes a new page in the observation logbook.

Follow Up

When the life cycle is complete, add a page to the class logbook entitled "Beetle Life Cycle." Reproduce copies of page 5 for students to write about what they did, what they saw, and what they learned as they raised the beetles. You may want to introduce the term metamorphosis at this time. (Metamorphosis is a major form change during the life cycle stages of an animal.)

Egg to Butterfly

Raise butterflies in the classroom. Observe and record the changes that occur.

Materials

- terrarium
- netting and string
- twigs (from plant where you collected the eggs or caterpillar)
- eggs or caterpillars

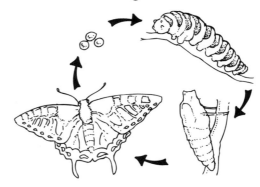

Steps to Follow

1. Prepare a recordkeeping chart on a large sheet of chart or butcher paper.

Butterfly Life Cycle		
date	observer's name	changes
May 4	Sarah	The caterpillars are eating leaves.
May 6	Jason	Three caterpillars molted.

2. Put several twigs and 4–6 eggs or caterpillars in the terrarium. (Check the undersides of leaves to locate eggs or caterpillars.)
3. Cover the container with netting or fine screening. Tie it securely with string.
4. Provide fresh food daily, removing any left from the previous day. (Use leaves from the same type of plant on which you found the eggs or caterpillars.)
5. Observe changes and record on the chart. Gently measure length of the caterpillars, record the number of moltings, record the day the caterpillar forms a chrysalis, and the day the adult comes out of chrysalis.

The day you release the adult butterflies, add a page entitled "Butterfly Life Cycle" to the class logbook. Reproduce copies of the logbook form on page 5 for students to write about what they did, what they saw, and what they learned as they raised the butterflies. Review the term metamorphosis.

Gather More Information

- Reproduce the "Invertebrates Change and Grow" minibook on pages 42–44 for each student. Read the minibook together to review invertebrate life cycles.

- Share books about life cycles such as *Snails* by Jens Olesen (Silver Burdett, 1986), *The Ladybug* by Sabrina Crew (Raintree Steck-Vaughn, 1997), and *Octopus* by Carol Carrick (Clarion Books, 1978).

- Reproduce one or more life cycle sequencing activities (pages 45–47). Students cut out and glue the pictures in sequence. Extend the activity by having students write a paragraph describing the changes that occur during the life cycle.

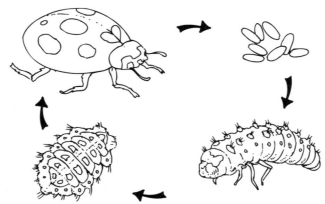

- Have students use the information they have learned about invertebrate life cycles to write a definition of "Life Cycle" for the class logbook.

  Reproduce copies of the logbook form on page 4 for each student. Have them copy the definition for their individual logbooks.

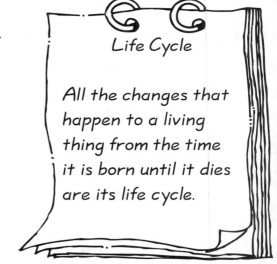

Life Cycle

All the changes that happen to a living thing from the time it is born until it dies are its life cycle.

Mealworm to Beetle

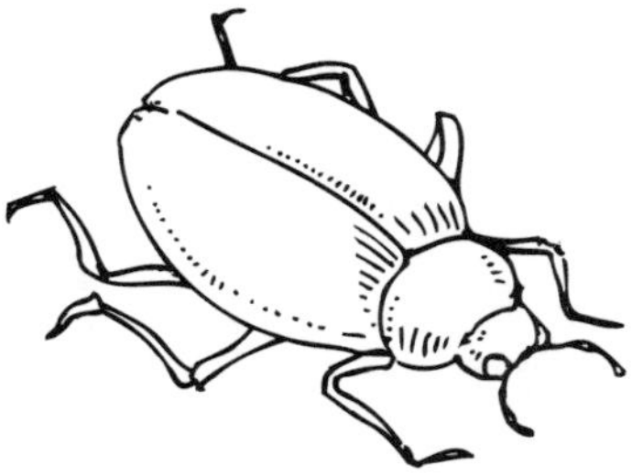

Date: _____

Observer: _____

What the mealworms are doing:

_____

_____

_____

_____

Draw a mealworm here.

Animals without Backbones • EMC 855

Name _____

Invertebrates Change and Grow

All invertebrates are born, grow up, reproduce, and die. This is a **life cycle**. Some babies look like their parents when they are born.

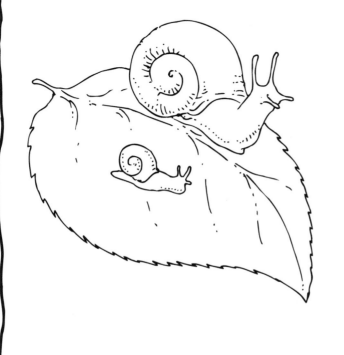

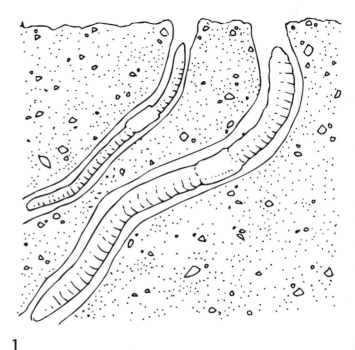

Some babies are very different. They will change a lot as they grow up. This big change is called **metamorphosis** (met uh mor' fuh sis).

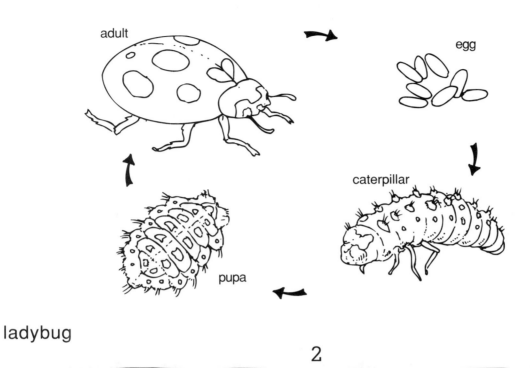

adult

egg

caterpillar

pupa

ladybug

A female spider lays many eggs at a time.
She wraps the eggs in a ball of silk.
When the babies hatch they are called **spiderlings.**

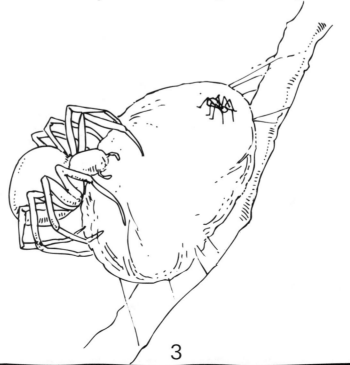

A female snail lays her eggs in the ground.
When the babies hatch they are tiny, but they already look like snails.

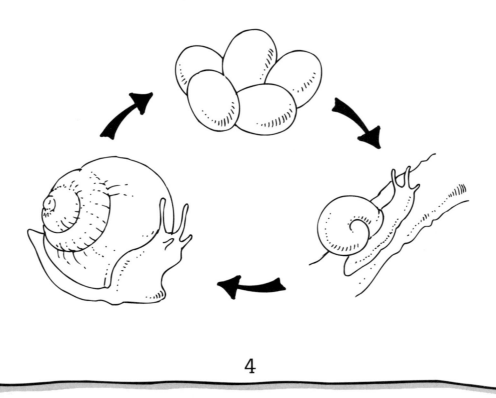

4

A female lobster carries her eggs until they are ready to hatch. A baby lobster does not look like its mother. It drifts near the top of the water. It molts its tiny shell several times. Then it looks more like a lobster.

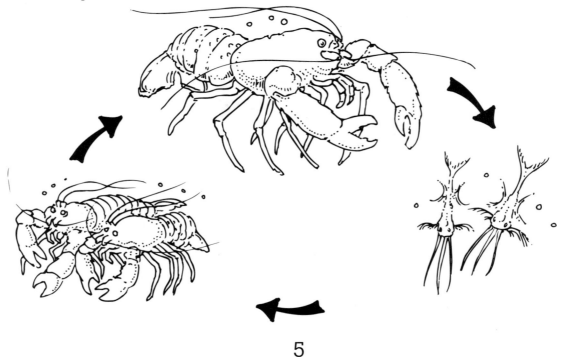

5

Name _____

Cut out the pictures.
Paste them in order.

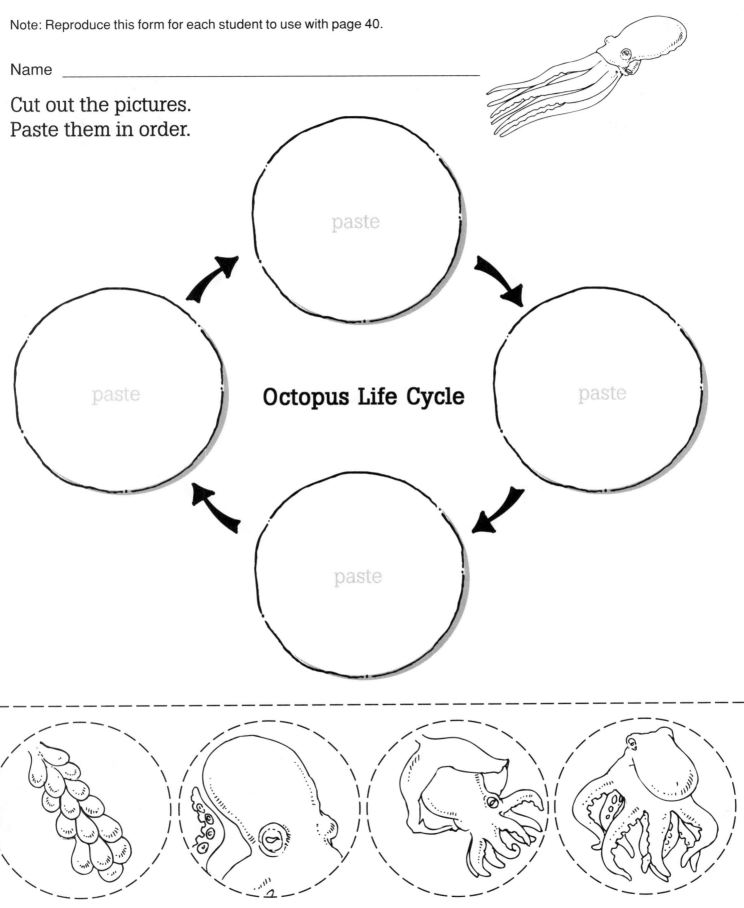

Octopus Life Cycle

paste

paste

paste

paste

Note: Reproduce this form for each student to use with page 40.

Name _____

Cut out the pictures.
Paste them in order.

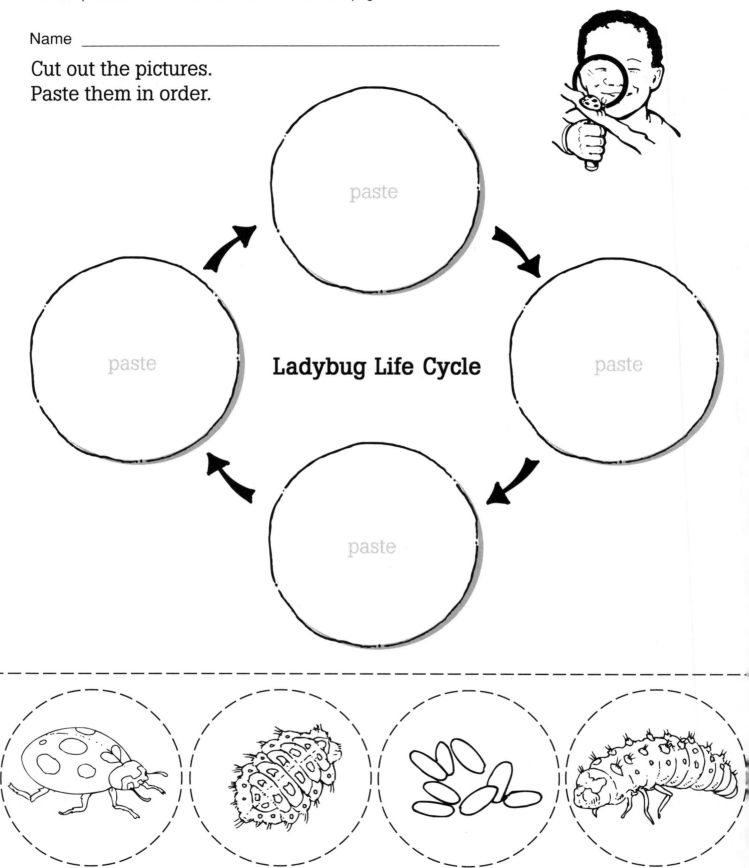

Ladybug Life Cycle

paste

paste

paste

paste

Animals without Backbones • EMC 855

Name _____

Cut out the pictures.
Paste them in order.

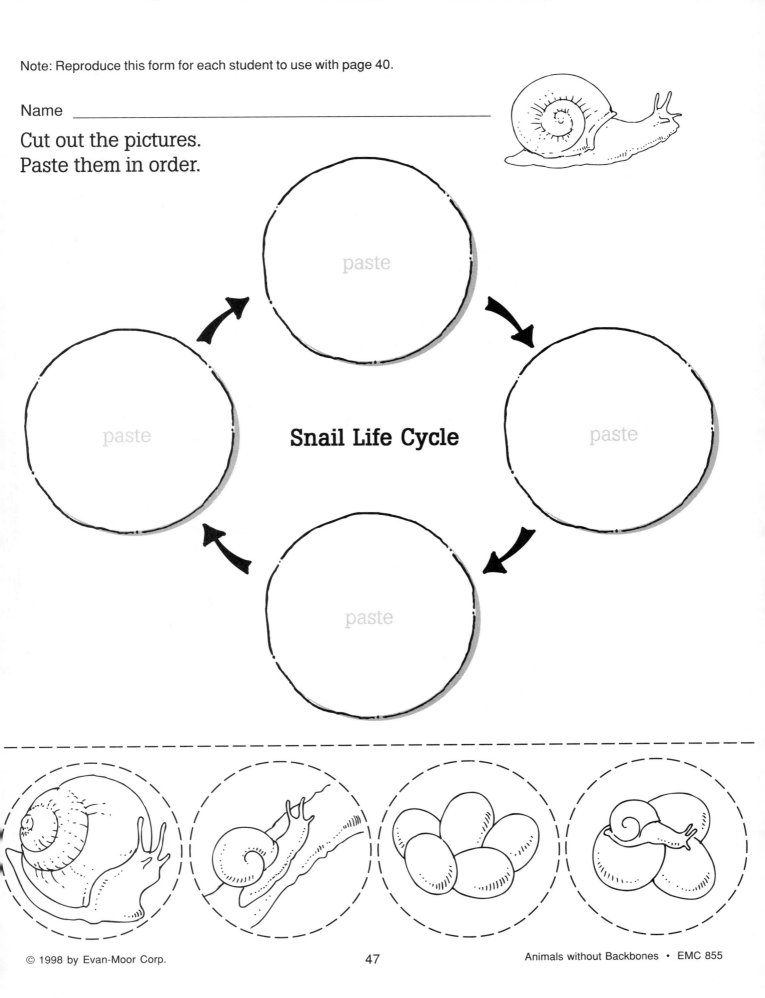

Snail Life Cycle

paste

paste

paste

paste

Invertebrates have developed different ways of acquiring food.

How Do They Eat?

- Engage students in a discussion of how they find food when they're hungry. *(I look for it in the kitchen. I smell the things my mom is cooking and ask her if I can have some. I get something out of the refrigerator.)* Explain that they have used some of their five senses to find food. Ask questions to get students to identify the senses they used.

- Divide the class into small groups. Have the groups observe how each kind of classroom invertebrate locates and eats its food. Have students share what they observe.

- Add a page to the class logbook entitled "How Our Animals Eat."

Reproduce the logbook form on page 4 for each student to use to record what they learned.

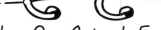

How Our Animals Eat

Earthworms wiggle around to find food. They drag leaves into their tunnels.

Snails use their feelers to find food. They crawl on slimy trails to food. They chew the leaves.

Ants run around. They touch stuff with their antennae. They bite with their jaws.

Our spider spins a web. It waits for a fly to get caught.

How Do Wild Animals Find Food?

- Brainstorm to list ways animals without backbones might get their food. You may need to ask questions to get the students started. "How do you think a grasshopper gets its food? How about a crab? A barnacle is stuck to a rock. How do you think it gets food?" Record their ideas on a page entitled "Finding Food" for the class logbook. Write all their ideas. Corrections and additions will be made later.

- Make an overhead transparency of page 52, showing various types of invertebrates getting food. Use the pictures to help students identify physical adaptations that assist animals in collecting and eating food. Point to one picture at a time and ask questions such as, "What is the snail eating? What helps the snail eat the plant leaf?" Continue questioning as you view each picture.

  Reproduce copies of the logbook form on page 4 for students to complete for their individual logbooks.

- Read books such as *The Hunt for Food* by Anita Gareri (Millbrook Press, 1997), *When Hunger Calls* by Bert Kitchen (Candlewick Press, 1994), or *Time to Eat: Animals Who Hide and Save Their Food* by Marilyn Ballie (Firefly Books Ltd., 1995). Or watch a video of animals as they gather or catch food. Ask students to recall what they learned. Make additions and corrections to the class logbook.

"Finding Food" Minibook

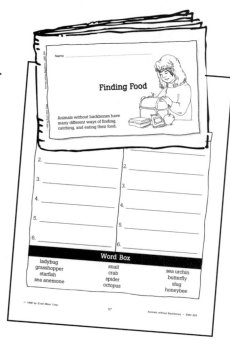

- Reproduce the minibook on pages 53–56 for each student. Read the book together to review how invertebrates find and eat their food.

- Reproduce page 57 for each student. They are to divide the animals listed into meat eaters and plant eaters.

Extension Activities

What Do Snails Eat?

Have students discuss what types of things they think a snail might like to eat. Then do the following experiment.

Materials

- different kinds of leaves and flowers, bits of raw vegetables, peanut butter, crackers
- paper plates
- snails
- plastic spoons
- copies of page 5, reproduced for each student

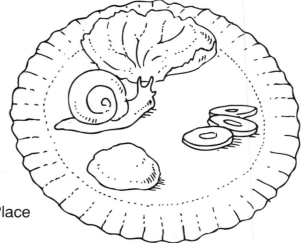

Steps to Follow

1. Divide the class into pairs or small groups.
2. Have each group put three items on a paper plate. Place the snail in the center of the plate.
3. Observe the snail and record what happens.
4. When the allotted time is up, have each group share what they discovered.

Follow Up

Ask students to explain why people become upset when they find snails in their gardens.

What Do Ants Eat?

Explain to students that they are going to help you discover an ant's favorite food.

Materials

- an ant home in a baking pan (see page 15)
- four strips of construction paper
- four small blocks of wood
- four jar lids
- copies of page 5, reproduced for each student
- an assortment of human foods in tiny amounts (peanut butter, chocolate, salt, baking soda, sugar, crushed peanuts, potato chips, hamburger, bread, cooked egg, mayonnaise, ketchup, etc.)

Steps to Follow

Have students assist as you:

1. Space the four wood blocks evenly around the ant home and place a jar lid on each block.
2. Fold the paper the long way until it forms a stiff ramp that the ants can climb down. Fold over one end of the paper ramp and place it in the top of the ant home so it touches the soil. Cut the ramp so the other end reaches into the jar lid.
3. Put a small amount of different human foods in each jar lid. Change the types of foods every day or so.
4. Observe the ants for several days. Reproduce copies of the logbook form on page 5 for each student to record what they learned.
5. Ask students to describe what they saw. Facilitate the discussion by asking questions such as these:

   "Do the ants like one human food best?"

   "Are there some foods that the ants don't like?"

Follow Up

Pose these questions: "How do ants know where to find food? How does one ant tell another where food is located?" Read *Ants* by Ruth Berman (The Lerner Publishing Group, 1996), or *Ants* by Karen Hartley and Chris Marco (Heinemann Library, 1998) to help students answer these questions.

Some Ways Invertebrates Eat

Name _____

Finding Food

Animals without backbones have many different ways of finding, catching, and eating their food.

1

Animals use their different senses to locate food.

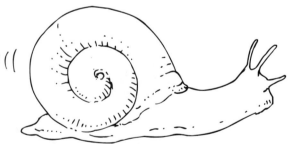 

Many insects and some spiders have good eyesight. This helps them find food.

Many small animals use feet, **tentacles** (ten' tuh kulz), or **antennae** (an ten' ee) to feel around for food. Some also smell and taste with their feet or antennae.

Other animals feel the ground or water moving or hear sound when their prey comes close.

2

Some animals fly, crawl, hop, swim, or walk around looking for plants to eat. Some eat plant leaves. Some sip nectar from flowers.

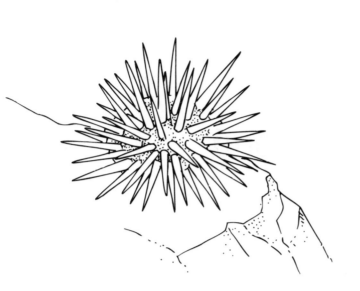

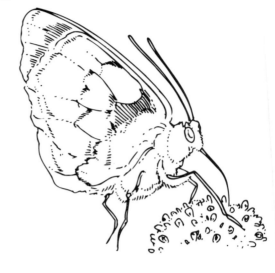

Some even eat rotting plants and animals.

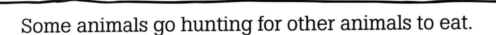

3

Some animals go hunting for other animals to eat.

Spitting spiders shoot glue from their fangs.
Moon snails eat sand dollars.
Ladybugs go after aphids (a' fidz).
Anemones catch small fish.

spitting spider

4

Some animals set traps and wait for food to come by. Then they pounce!

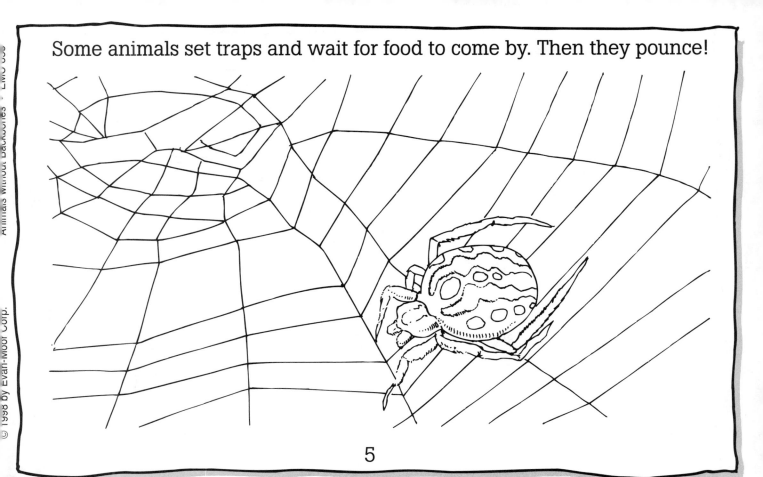

5

There are many animals in the ocean that never move or only move a little. These animals have to sit and wait for food to come to them.

barnacles

Filter feeders take small plants and animals out of water as it flows into and out of their bodies.

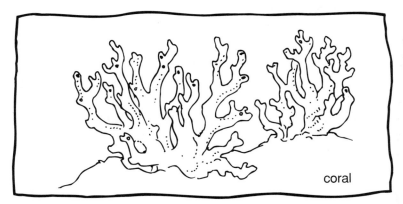

coral

6

There are some insects that store food for later.

Bees make and store honey.

Leaf-cutter ants grow their own food. The ants take pieces of leaves to their nest. They use the leaves to grow a plant called fungus. They eat the fuzzy fungus.

7

Many animals have special parts that help them get their food or eat it.

Snails have a rough tongue for eating leaves.

An octopus has suction cups to help hold its prey.

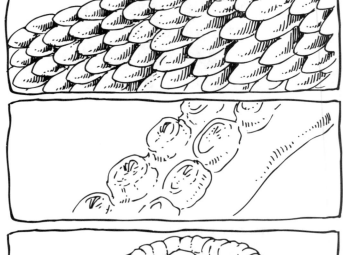

Sea urchins have five sharp teeth for scraping seaweed off rocks.

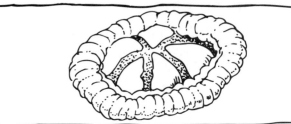

8

Note: Reproduce this form for each student to use with page 49.

Name _____

What Do We Eat?

Write the names under the kind of food each animal eats.

We eat meat.	We eat parts of plants.
1. _____	1. _____
2. _____	2. _____
3. _____	3. _____
4. _____	4. _____
5. _____	5. _____
6. _____	6. _____

Word Box

ladybug	snail	sea urchin
grasshopper	crab	butterfly
sea star	spider	slug
sea anemone	octopus	honeybee

Animals without Backbones • EMC 855

Invertebrates' movements are adapted to the animals' needs.

How Do I Move?

- Begin by observing the movements of the invertebrates in your classroom terrariums. Ask students to describe and give a name to the type of movement each makes. *(Earthworms crawl. They stretch out the front end and pull up the back end. Ants walk and run on their legs.)*

Gently place the snail from your terrarium on a piece of black paper. Observe the silver trail a snail makes. Some students may want to let a snail crawl across their hands to feel the movement and the slimy trail the snail leaves. (Have soap and paper towels on hand for handwashing when you are finished.)

- Use questions to help students recall other animals without backbones and how they move. Ask, "Can anyone tell me the name of another insect? How does it move? Who can name an animal with a hard outside that lives in the ocean? How does it move?"

Record all their ideas on a chart entitled "How Invertebrates Move" for the class logbook. You will make additions and corrections later.

How Invertebrates Move

Earthworms crawl.

Ants walk and run.

Snails slide on a sticky trail.

Crabs walk on many legs.

Starfish crawl.

An octopus swims through the water.

Animals without Backbones • EMC 855

Gather More Information

- Read appropriate parts of *Animals in Action* (Time Life, 1989) or view videos to learn more about the ways invertebrates move. Make additions and corrections to the class logbook. Reproduce copies of the logbook form on page 4 for each student. They are to write about invertebrate movements for their individual logbooks.

- Reproduce the "How Invertebrates Move" minibook on pages 61–64 for each student. Read the pages together to review ways invertebrates move. Make additions or corrections to the class logbook page.

Comparing Vertebrate and Invertebrate Movements

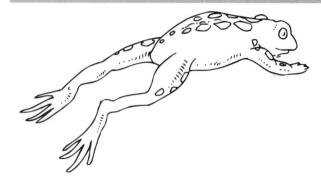
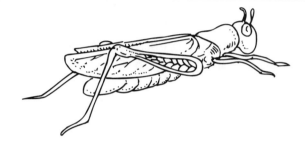

Compare movements of vertebrates and invertebrates. Give an example of a vertebrate and ask how it moves. Then have students name one or more invertebrates that can move the same way.

"How does a bird move?" *(fly)*

"Name animals without backbones that can fly." *(bee, grasshopper, fly)*

"How can a monkey move?" *(climb, walk, run)*

"Name an animal without a backbone that can climb. *(octopus)*

"Name an animal without a backbone that can walk." *(spider)*

"Name an animal without a backbone that can run." *(ant)*

After making many comparisons, give each student a sheet of drawing paper. They are to fold the paper in half. On one half they are to draw a vertebrate that is moving. On the other half they are to draw an invertebrate making the same movement. Have them name each animal and how it is moving. Staple the pages in a cover to make a class book.

A snake can slither.   A worm can, too.

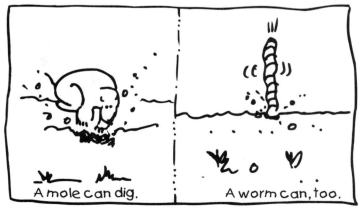

A mole can dig.   A worm can, too.

Explore Invertebrate Movements

- Octopuses, squid, and jellyfish all use some form of jet propulsion to move quickly through the water. Have students model jet propulsion using balloons to represent the siphon and air to represent water.

  Have students blow up their balloons and hold the ends shut to keep in the air. Do a countdown and have students release the balloons. Collect the balloons, and then ask students to explain how this is like the way an octopus moves.

  Reproduce the logbook form on page 5 for students to record what they did, what they saw, and what they learned for their individual logbooks.

- Octopuses have suction cups on their arms. Flies have suction cups on their feet. Bring in small suction cups so students can explore how they work. (You can buy suction cups at hardware and kitchen supply stores.) Ask students to explain how having suction cups on feet or arms could help an animal move.

  Reproduce the logbook form on page 4 for each student. They are to write about how suction cups help animals move.

- In a large empty area have students try to move in the ways of some invertebrates:

  crawl along on stomach like a worm or snail
  leap as far as possible from squatting position like a grasshopper
  walk like a crab or lobster on hands and feet
  pull self along with hands in the way an octopus uses its arms
  turn a somersault like an anemone

Name _____

How Invertebrates Move

On land or in the water, animals without backbones move in many ways.

1

Invertebrates with no legs can move.

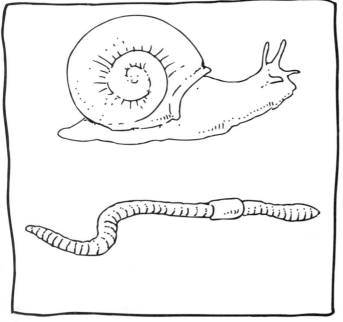

Worms and snails crawl on land.

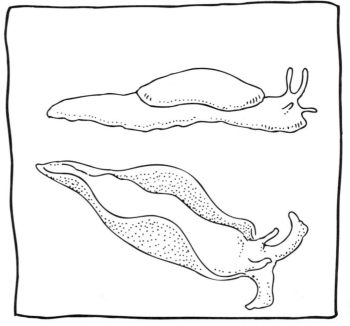

Snails and slugs crawl in the water.
Some slugs wiggle their side flaps
to swim.

2

Invertebrates with six or ten legs can move.

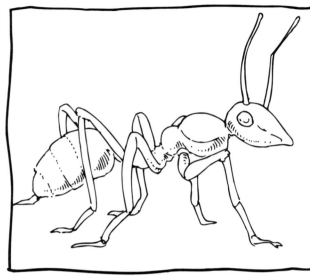

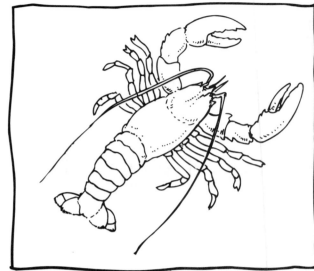

Insects have six legs. They run, jump, hop, or fly.

Lobsters, crabs, and shrimp have more than six legs. They have eight legs for walking and two with claws. Some of them walk and some swim.

3

Invertebrates with eight arms or legs can move.

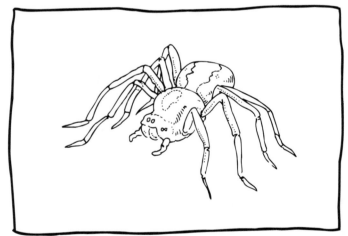

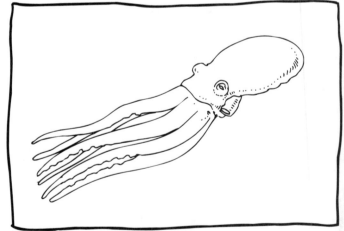

Spiders have eight legs. They walk around. They pounce on prey. Sometimes they float through the air on a line of silk.

Octopus have eight arms (**tentacles**). They crawl over rocks using suction cups on their arms. They swim by twisting their arms. They push water out of a funnel (**siphon**) to jet through the water.

4

Animals with many legs can move.

Centipedes have many legs. They use their legs to walk and run.

Starfish and sea urchins have hundreds of little feet called tube feet. There are tiny suction cups on the ends of the feet.

5

In the ocean, some animals move in unusual ways.

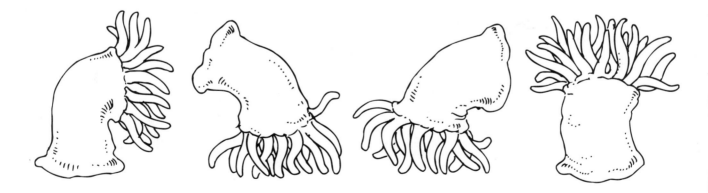

An anemone turns a somersault to move from place to place.

6

Honeybees move in a special way. They do a dance to tell other bees how to find food.

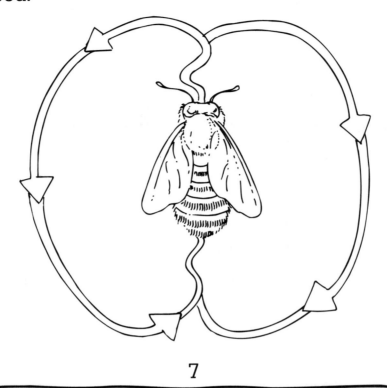

7

And some animals without backbones don't move at all.

barnacles

8

Invertebrates have developed many forms of self-defense.

Animal Defenses

- Begin a discussion of animals' defenses by asking students to recall what their pets do when they are frightened. *(My dog barks and snarls. My cat runs and hides under the bed. Sometimes my cat uses its claws to scratch. My canary makes a lot of noise and flaps her wings. My lizard sits very still on its rock. Sometimes it runs under the rock.)*

- Continue the discussion by having students observe what the classroom invertebrates do. *(A snail goes into its shell. The earthworms hide in their tunnels. The ants run around, and then go into their tunnels. Ants will bite. The spider runs and hides. Spiders will bite, too.)*

- Brainstorm with students the ways other invertebrates protect themselves. You may need to ask questions to get students started.

> "We saw our snails hide in their shells. Can you think of other invertebrates we've learned about that hide in shells?"
> "Can you name invertebrates that hide in other ways?"
> "Some of you said ants and spiders bite. Besides biting, what other ways do some invertebrates defend themselves?

Record these on a page entitled "Animal Defenses" for the class logbook.

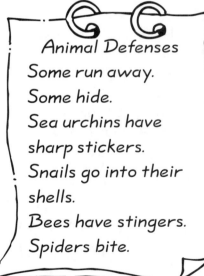

Animal Defenses
Some run away.
Some hide.
Sea urchins have
sharp stickers.
Snails go into their
shells.
Bees have stingers.
Spiders bite.

- Read books such as *Animals' Defenses* by Jeremy Cherfas (the Learner Publishing Group, 1991), *What Color Is Camouflage?* by Carolyn Otto (HarperCollins Children's Books, 1996), or *Eyewitness Junior Books Amazing Animal Disguises* by Sandie Sowler (Alfred A. Knopf, 1982) and *Amazing Armored Animals* by Sandie Sowler (Alfred A. Knopf, 1992). Ask students to recall what they learned from the readings. Teach the terms protective coloration, camouflage, and mimicry.

Camouflage, Protective Coloration, Mimicry

- Reproduce page 68. You will need one picture per student. Challenge students to use color or design to create an insect that can be "hidden" in the classroom.

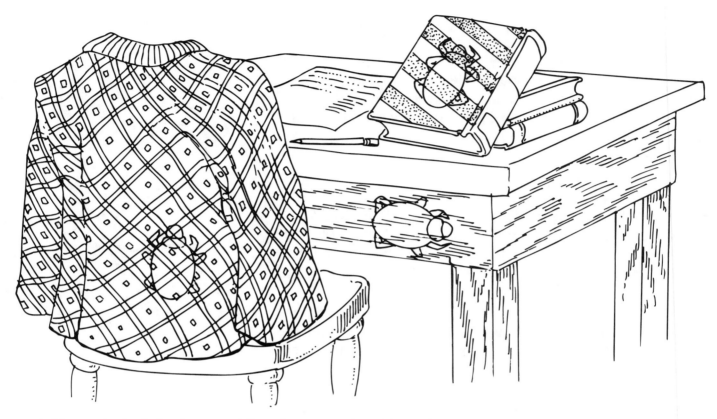

1. Have students look around the classroom for places they might put their animal when it is finished (on a wall, colored paper on a bulletin board, a patterned object such as a vase, someone's lunch box, the teacher's favorite plaid shirt, etc.). Remind students of how color, pattern, and mimicry can protect an animal.

2. Have students select a location and write it on the back of the animal. Then, have them color the animal and hand it in.

  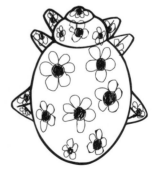

3. When all the animals have been collected, pin or tape the animals in their designated locations while students are out of the classroom.

4. Students are to try to locate the animals.

5. After an allotted amount of time, discuss which animals were the most difficult to find and why.

 Animals without Backbones • EMC 855

Gather More Information

- Reproduce the minibook on pages 69–71 for each student. Read the book together to review the various types of vertebrate defenses. Have students complete the book.

- Add new information to the class's "Animal Defenses" logbook and make any corrections to previous information. Reproduce the logbook form on page 4 for students to write about animal defenses for their individual logbooks.

- Go outside and look for invertebrates hiding in plants around the school grounds. Have students look carefully at the undersides of leaves, among plant matter on the ground, on the bark of trees, etc. to see if they can find invertebrates using any of the forms of protection they have learned about. Have students share what they found.

  Reproduce copies of the logbook form on page 5 for students to write about what they did, what they saw, and what they learned.

- Invite a biologist or naturalist to speak to the class about invertebrate defenses. Ask the speaker to bring along live examples or photographs of invertebrates to share with the students.

Summary Activities

- Reproduce pages 72 and 73 for each student.

  Have students find the animals hiding in the picture on page 72. Have them match the animals on page 73 with their kinds of self defense.

- Give each student a sheet of drawing paper and a sheet of writing paper. Students are to select one form of self-defense used by invertebrates and then draw the invertebrate and write about how it protects itself.

 Animals without Backbones • EMC 855

68

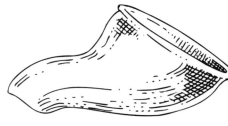

Invertebrate Defenses

Animals without backbones have many different kinds of self-defense.

1

Some fight back if they are attacked. Some have poison. Some smell bad.

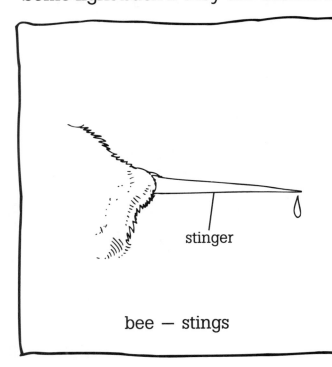

stinger

bee — stings

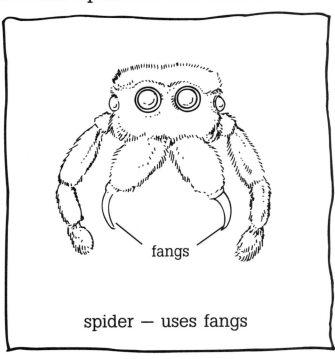

fangs

spider — uses fangs

2

Some animals are good at looking like something else.

This katydid looks like a leaf.

This cockroach looks like a bad-tasting ladybug.

3

There are many animals with bright colors. These colors are a warning that say, "Don't eat me. I taste bad." Other animals learn not to eat these bad-tasting animals.

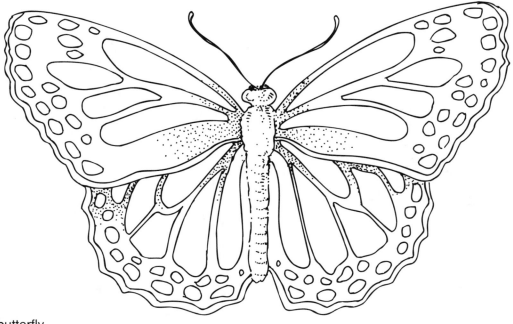

Monarch butterfly

4

Other animals can change their color or pattern quickly to match the background. This helps them hide from predators.

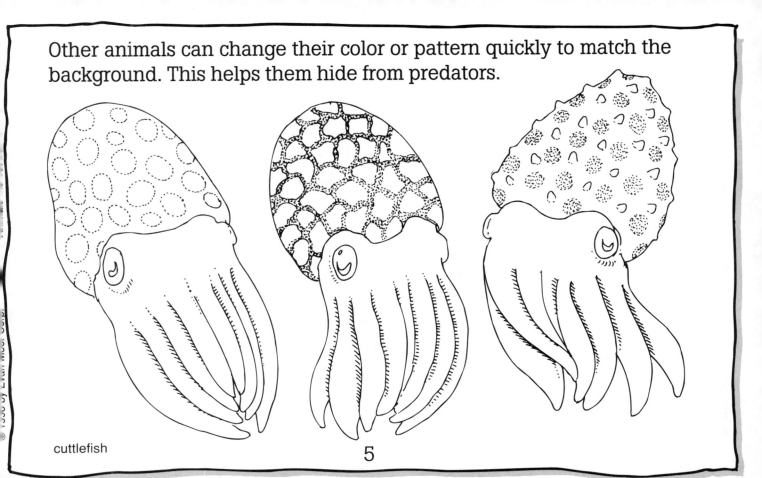

cuttlefish

5

Some animals have hard shells. These help protect the soft animal inside.

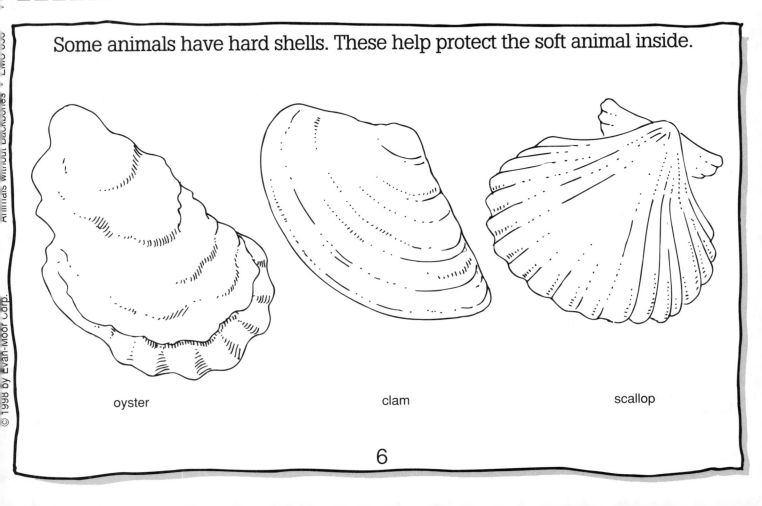

oyster   clam   scallop

6

Name _____

Find the Animals

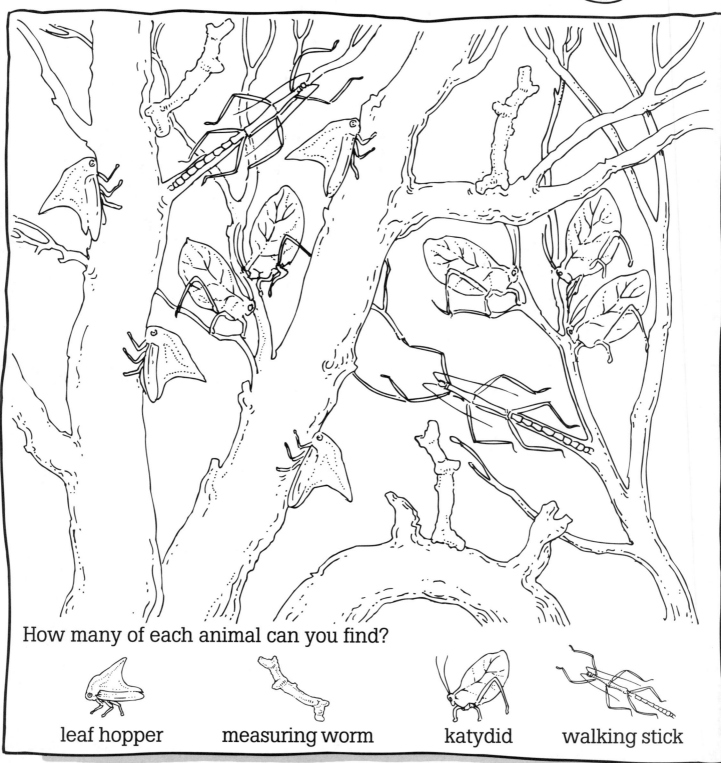

How many of each animal can you find?

leaf hopper   measuring worm   katydid   walking stick

Animals without Backbones • EMC 855

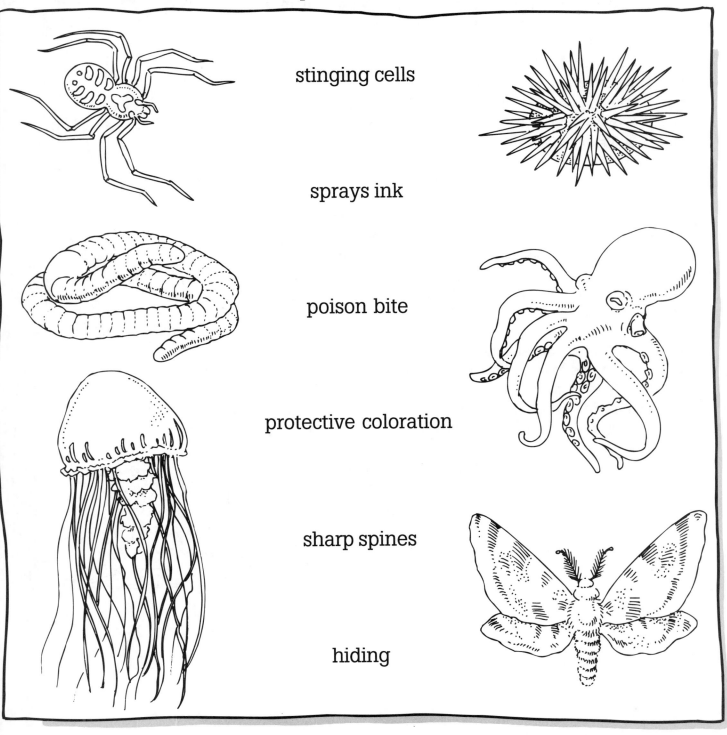

Note: Reproduce this form for each student to use with page 67.

Name _____

What I Use for Protection

Match the animal to the kind of protection it is uses.

stinging cells

sprays ink

poison bite

protective coloration

sharp spines

hiding

Animals without Backbones • EMC 855

Some invertebrates build homes.

What Is a Home?

• Encourage students to give reasons why they live in homes. Write their ideas on the chalkboard.

> A home is where we eat.
> We need a place to sleep.
> A home keeps us safe.
> It's where our family can be together.
> A home is where we work and play.
> A home keeps us warm if it's snowing.
> A home keeps us dry if it's raining.

• Have students observe the classroom animals. Ask , "What kinds of homes do our animals live in? *(terrarium, jar, aquarium)* Why are homes important for pet animals like these in the classroom?" *(They need a place to be safe from danger. They need food and a place to sleep. They would get lost if they didn't have a home.)*

• Discuss whether wild animals need homes. Guide students with questioning to reach these conclusions:
> Many wild animals don't have homes.
> Some wild animals do build homes.
> Animals build homes to have a safe place to raise a family.

• Begin a class logbook page entitled "Invertebrate Homes." Reproduce the logbook form on page 4 for students to write about animals' homes for their individual logbooks.

Invertebrate Homes

Some animals build homes.

They want a place that is safe.

They want a place to raise babies.

Animals without Backbones • EMC 855

Invertebrate Builders

- Read appropriate parts of books such as *Books for Young Explorers — Animals That Build Their Homes* by Robert McClung (National Geographic Society, 1976) or *Animals' Homes* by Theodore Entwistle (Random House All-About Books, 1987) to learn about animal builders. Ask students to recall which animals built homes, what they used to make them, and how they used the homes (raised babies, stored food, for protection).

- If possible, bring in an empty beehive or wasp nest or use photographs from a trade book. If students are unable to name the object, provide the name. Ask students to think about how the home was made and how it was used.

  Explain that many invertebrate home builders live together in groups (ants, bees, termites). Ask students to think of reasons this might be helpful.

- Make additions to the class logbook page "Invertebrate Homes." Reproduce the logbook form on page 4 for students to write about invertebrate homes for their individual journals.

"Invertebrate Homes" Minibook

Reproduce pages 76–80 for each student.
Read the pages together to review facts about animal builders.

Make a Report

Divide the class into small groups. Assign each group a type of invertebrate home (ant, bee, wasp, worm, trap-door spider). Each group is to work together to paint a picture of the animal and its home. They are to write a paragraph describing the home and explaining how the animal uses the home. Provide books with good photographs for students to use as they create their pictures.

Provide time for one student from each group to share the pictures and paragraphs with the class.

Invertebrate Homes

1

Most invertebrates don't have homes. They don't need a special place to stay. They go around looking for food. They sleep wherever they are. They have their babies wherever they are.

anemone

crab

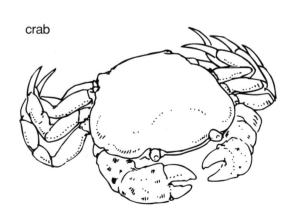

2

Some invertebrates do build homes. They build homes to be safe. They build homes to raise their babies. These bees have built a hive. They store food in the hive. They raise babies in the hive.

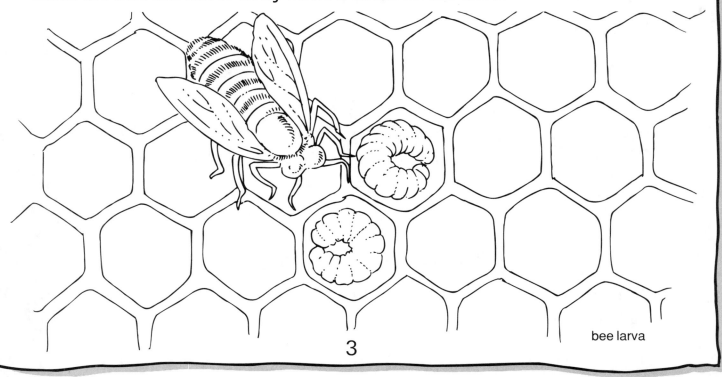

bee larva

3

Wasps and mud daubers built nests, too.

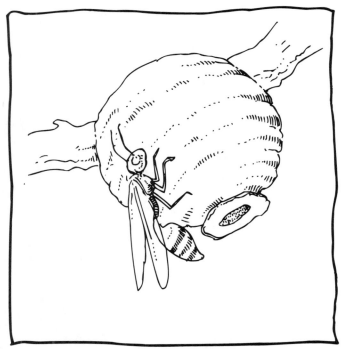 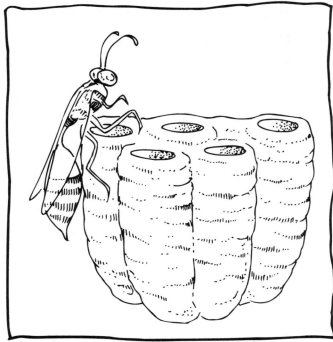

4

Ants live together in large homes. They build tunnels and rooms. They store food in some rooms. They hatch eggs and raise babies in other rooms.

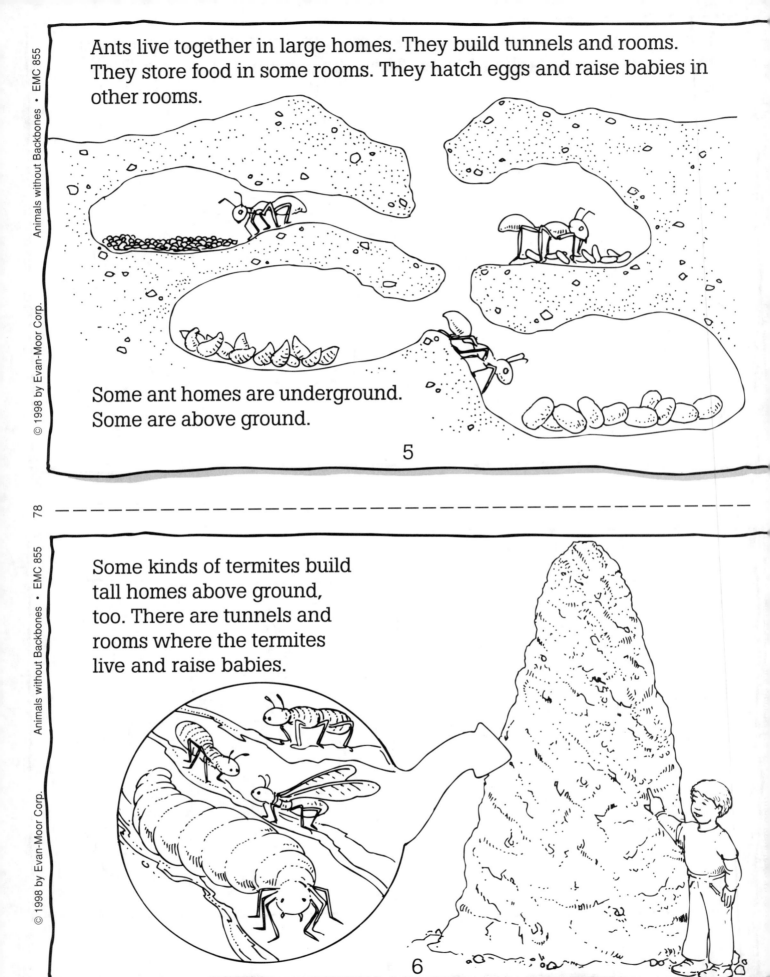

Some ant homes are underground.
Some are above ground.

5

Some kinds of termites build tall homes above ground, too. There are tunnels and rooms where the termites live and raise babies.

6

A trap-door spider builds a tunnel. It lines the tunnel with silk. It waits at the door to catch food. It raises baby spiders in the tunnel.

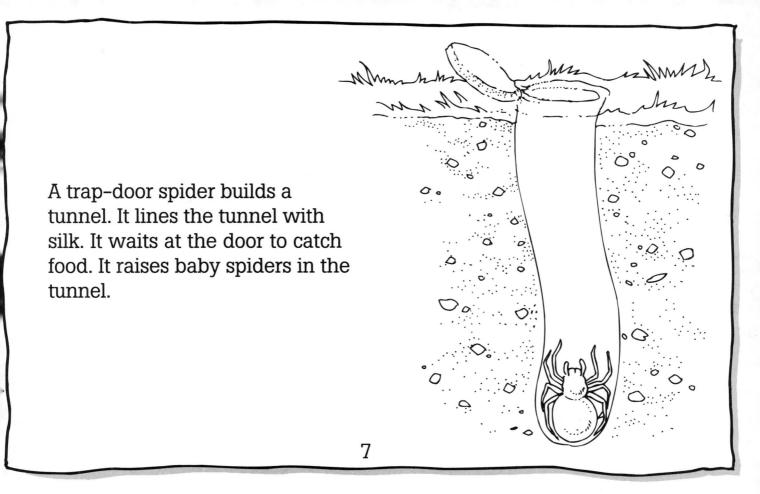

Earthworms live in tunnels they dig underground.

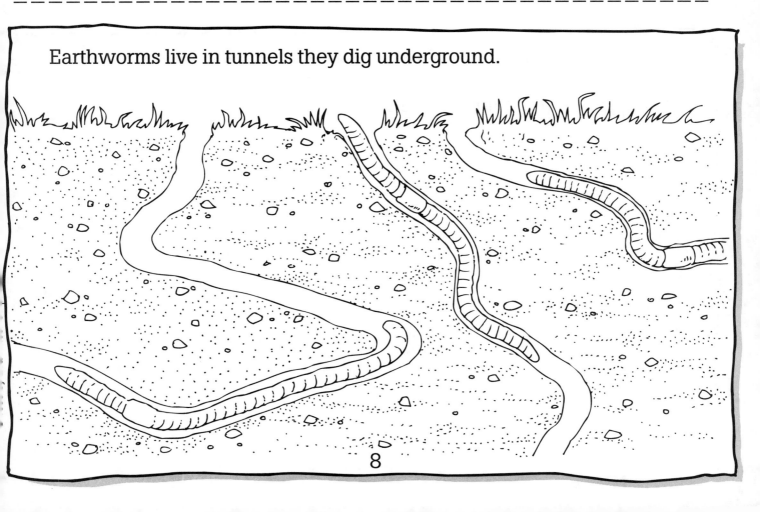

Some animals carry their homes with them. Snails on land and snails in the water make their own shells.

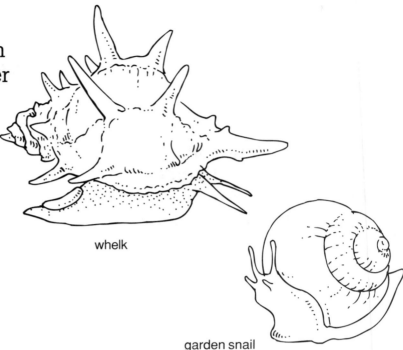

whelk

moon snail

garden snail

Clams, oysters, and scallops don't move around, but they have shells to live in.

9

Hermit crabs borrow their homes. They do not make their own shells like other crabs. They crawl into empty snail shells. When they grow too big for their homes, they find bigger shells.

10

ScienceWorks for Kids

Additional Science Resource Books

Big Book Stories & Reproducible Minibooks
Integrate science and reading. Each 11" x 17" book has 8 black & white fully-illustrated stories, each with a reproducible minibook. 64 pp. each. Grades K-2.

How to Do Science Experiments with Children
Teacher instructions and student record sheets for 75 experiments and demonstrations. Concepts include air, sound, water, electricity, light, and chemistry. 240 pp. Grades 1-3. EMC 846

Hands-On Science—Themes for the Whole Year
10 hands-on themes—teacher instructions and reproducible student lab books. Sound, Magnets, Aquarium, Sink & Float, Bubbles & Air, Color, Cold & Heat, Foods, Plants, Mealworms & Snails. 96 pp. Grades 1-3. EMC 828

Science & Math—How to Make Books with Children Series
Create student-authored books on 36 science topics and 14 math topics. Step-by-step directions and reproducible writing forms and patterns. 160 pp. Grades 1-6. EMC 298

How to Write Simple Science Reports
Reproducible forms and illustrations, writing suggestions, discussion starters, and science information. 30 reports in the categories of wild animals, animal homes, and prehistoric animals. 128 pp. Grades 1-4. EMC 395

Big Book of Science Rhymes and Chants
32 rhymes and chants to teach science concepts. Each one is on a separate page with illustrations that are among Evan-Moor's best. 64 pp. Grades K-2. EMC 306

Giant Science Resource Book
It's all in here: picture cards, diagrams, graphic organizers, and student activity sheets; organized by science topics—life science, physical science, earth science, space science, and environmental science. 304 pp. Grades 1-6. EMC 398

Science Picture Cards
24 full-color, 8 1/2" x 11" cards; science information on backs of cards.

(frog, robin, skunk, butterfly, grasshopper)

EMC 855

Evan-Moor
EDUCATIONAL PUBLISHERS